HOW TO BE A VIDEO INTERVIEW PRO

25 Strategies to Get ATTENTION and Make Your YouTube, Livestream, Google Hangouts, Skype Interviews and Videos Look or Professional TV or

D1502554

by Mike Koenigs a... ...

How to Be a Video Interview Pro: 25 Strategies to Get ATTENTION and Make Your YouTube, Livestream, Google Hangouts, Skype Interviews and Videos Look or Sound Like a Professional TV or Radio Show

Cover by Kristen Sibayan

Custom Art by Yanglyn Ou

ISBN-13: 9781511781060

ISBN-10: 1511781068

Book Website

www.VideoInterviewBook.com

Feedback or Suggestions? Errors or mistakes?

Send them to: Support@Mixiv.com

Printed in U.S.A

Get the "25 Strategies Book" as an Infographic and Video

This book is also available as a training video and handy infographic that you can print out and post next to your computer or share with someone you want to interview.

To get it, text your email address to:

+1 (858) 877-9700 or visit:

www.VideoInterviewBook.com

Endorsements and Accolades

"There are those who lead and those who follow and then there are trend creators. Mike is the latter who uses his creative genius and relentless pursuit of new frontiers and technologies to change the landscape of what is possible and usable in today's crazy, ever-changing business landscape."

John Assaraf, NY Times Bestselling Author, Founder PraxisNow.com

"I feel very blessed to have Mike Koenigs as a friend and in my personal and business life. After many years of teaching people around the world, it is guys like Mike Koenigs that keeps me sharp. And, we both share the same goals of wanting to help millions of entrepreneurs achieve their goals to greater financial and business success. More people need to engage in Mike's teachings – quite amazing!"

Brian Tracy, Author, Speaker, Entrepreneur

"There are very few visionaries who can truly look into the future and pluck from thin air the next big thing, not just once, but time after time - Tom Peters, Faith Popcorn, Sean Parker. Mike Koenigs breathes that rarified air. He's done it no less than eleven times over the past 20 years. But, unlike most, Mike not only sees the future, he monetizes it. In each of those eleven cases he took his vision and turned it into a successful million dollar plus business in fewer than 100 days. Whether he is teaching based on actual results (not theory), simplifying complex systems into digestible bites, extracting the genius from interviews with the most interesting people in the world or selling millions in front of the camera, I can think of no one better equipped to share with you the actionable knowledge Mike has distilled into his latest book."

Roland Frasier - CEO, All Channels Media

"Building a business or product takes a lot of work and is usually too daunting so most of us fail. But then there is Mike Koenigs. I have never seen anyone else have such a passion and ability to automate, teach and simplify any business process. He helps turn anyone into a superstar business stud. Thanks Mike!"

Eric Berman, CEO of Brandetize

"Mike Koenigs and I are in a mastermind group together and I have known him for several years. He is without question one of the smartest marketers I know. He's also one of the most deliberate, studied, systematic, focused and scientific entrepreneurs I know. I would recommend anything Mike produces because it is always top quality and delivers massive value. When it comes to business, he's the guy you want to be when you grow up :)"

Glen Ledwell CEO & Co Founder, Mind Movies LLC

"Mike never ceases to amaze me with his ability to spot and capitalize cutting edge business and marketing trends and then turn around and make it simple for anyone else to do the same. From the tools he creates to the training he provides, Mike knows what it takes to succeed quickly. As a bestselling publisher and consultant myself, I have often found myself asking "What would Mike Do?" Instead of reinventing the wheel, I simply steer it in his direction. Many people achieve success, only a few people can lead others to success as well as Mike Koenigs."

Brad Costanzo, CEO of Costanzo Marketing Group and Host of Bacon Wrapped Business

Foreword by *Overwhelmasaurus*

ROAR! Meet Disruptar.

Disruptar was abandoned as an egg.

He was taken into an orphanage.

And though he was cute and had a good heart, he grew very quickly into an extremely large, difficult to manage beast.

Disruptar was clumsy, awkward and labeled by peers and scientists alike a "Disruptasaurus."

But Disruptar knew he had something to offer the world—wisdom no one else had and everyone could use. (How to Survive Extinction When No One Else In Your Species Does, comes to mind). For years he struggled to try to find a way to get people's attention in some other way than just being laughed at.

Then one day, he found it. All he had to do was make some funny dinosaur faces and odd dinosaur noises and people laughed *with* him, not *at* him. Disruptar took this positive reinforcement and ran with it. He took his biggest flaws and turned them into superpowers and as a result, started teaching other people his secrets to getting and keeping attention.

Things were going great for Disruptar. He was sharing his wisdom, teaching his message, and feeling loved when he used to only feel ashamed.

But Disruptar eventually encountered another big challenge.

People started asking him to share his message all over the world... but if you've ever seen a dinosaur, they don't really travel well. He couldn't find a plane, train or automobile that could take him where his message was so desperately needed.

This broke Disruptar's heart and in his search for a solution, he found video interviewing. Excited at the possibility, Disruptar started doing interviews with Skype, Google Hangouts, Livestream and YouTube.

Much to his dismay, although the content was always 100% brilliant, he just couldn't get the video to look right. The angle made his teeth look too big, the sound was crackling, and the lighting made him look 100 million years old (instead of just 70 million). Worst of all, although he was always sure to look his interviewees in the eye, whenever he reviewed his video, he always seemed to be staring off into some unknown location.
Disruptar almost gave up.

And then he found Mike Koenigs.

Mike was teaching people (and dinosaurs) just like Disruptar how to get their messages out to more people with video. Mike was clearly a whiz at helping authors, experts, speakers, coaches, consultants, entrepreneurs and business owners get seen, heard, listened to and watched with technology, marketing and entertainment.

Disruptar immediately sent Mike a (poor quality) video asking for help.

And Mike, always eager to help the "underdog," or in this case the "underdino" agreed!

Mike had worked with lots of celebrity and bestselling author clients including Tony Robbins, Paula Abdul, the late Debbie Ford, John Assaraf, Brian Tracy, Jorge Cruise, Harvey Mackay, Richard Dreyfuss, Daniel Amen, JJ Virgin and Darren Hardy.

Mike had written 7 #1 bestselling books and after getting to know and love Disruptar (because he's such a lovable dinosaur) suggested Disruptar should write a book. Disruptar was scared to do it alone—so Mike suggested they co-author a book together to help other business owners get seen, heard and found.

This is their first project together.

Please be nice - it's Disruptar's first book and though he has thick, reptilian skin, he's still very sensitive.

But if you DO enjoy the book, please make sure you leave a five-star review on Amazon and download the "25 Strategies" video at www.Disruptasaurus.com

Sincerely,
Disruptar's best friend,
Overwhelmasaurus

PS - I hope Mike can help me write my first book next!

Table of Contents

Welcome - Read Me First!

Mike Koenigs
(**[M]** from now on)

Disruptar the Disruptasaurus
(**[D]** from now on)

[M]: Disruptar and I are going to share with you 25 ways to look great on camera, and make your YouTube, Livestream, Google Hangouts, Skype Interviews and Videos look like professional TV shows. It's my opinion that one of the most valuable skills you will ever learn is interviewing. Unfortunately, if you're like me, almost every interview you've ever watched or seen online looks horrible and sounds even worse. It's hard to take someone seriously when the background is distracting, or the video quality is poor, or the camera is aimed straight up the someone's nostrils. Gross, yet super common.

These small things make a big difference and though you see it in others' interviews, you've likely never noticed it about yourself. Problem is; everyone else does! And they're judging you. Big time. If you want someone to value you or your brand or your knowledge or the product you're selling them—you've gotta look like a million bucks on camera.

If your interviews look horrible, you and your products will be devalued. You're better than that—just like my friend Disruptar was better than that—and this book will make sure you look like a pro every time.

[D]: "Mike??

[M]: "Yes, Disruptar?"

[D]: "I hate for this to be the first contribution I make to this book, but I feel like it needs to be said: Your interviews aren't always perfect... are they? Don't you think you should tell them about what happened with Peter Diamandis?"

[M]: "Aw man. Do I have to?"

[D]: "Yes, Mike. I think you do."

[M]: Alright. Here's the truth. I too, have made some pretty crummy interviews and suffered the consequences. Not too long ago I had the honor of sitting down with someone I truly admire—Peter Diamandis.

He is the author of the NY Times Bestselling books ABUNDANCE, *BOLD* and the founder of XPRIZE. You know, the organization that brings the brightest minds together in an effort to out-invent each other; like, building rocket ships and sending people into space kind of inventions. This guy breaks all the rules and when he agreed to sit down with me and do an interview, I was out of my mind excited. Only problem? Peter was about to get on a plane and wasn't going to be available for two weeks (that's to be expected—we're both super busy people). But I was so excited, I broke some of my own rules.

You see, when I got the call from Peter, I wasn't in my studio where everything is set up perfectly according to these 25 tips. So I had to scramble a bit and when it came time for the interview, Peter said some earth-shattering, mind-blowing things (as usual) and it was amazing... and I looked *horrible!* It was pretty much unusable had it not been for my editors who were able to isolate my portion of the video and fix it in post-production (but most people don't have my team to fix stuff like this).

If I had just been thinking clearly, all I would have had to do was change two small things and it would have looked three times better. But instead, it looked horrible and I almost ruined an incredible opportunity. I would hate for you to suffer a similar fate, which is why we're here. Disruptar, Why don't you give them a quick glimpse of what they're getting in this content-packed book so they're prepared to make amazing video interviews every single time?

[D]: You got it, Mike. Here's what you have comin' your way my friend. We're gonna talk about strategy—it's a crowded, noisy distracted world out there. How do you grab their attention and keep it? (Don't worry, I gotcha covered on this one. They don't call me a Disruptasaurus for nothin'!) We'll give you the small hacks that make a big difference. Wanna lose 10 pounds in 10 seconds on camera?! That's Strategy #1! And we're also going to tell you *exactly* what equipment to use so you look like a first class television network for less than the cost of setting up your cable! ROAR!!!!

[M]: Whoa! Disruptar, keep it together, man!

[D]: Sorry, Mike. I can get a little carried away and roar when I get excited.

[M]: I get it, Disruptar. This is exciting stuff. But before we go any further, we should probably talk about platforms. That's really where it all starts. Even *before* the 25 strategies to make your YouTube, Livestream, Google Hangouts, Skype interviews and videos look like a professional TV Show....

[D]: Can I just ask... *Is that the most ridiculous title you've ever come up with Mike?*

[M]: *I wouldn't be talking about ridiculous if I were you, Disruptar.*

[D]: True. And you're right Mike, we should start with which platform you choose to record your interviews and videos. Skype? Google Hangouts? GotoMeeting? Oh My! Our preference? Skype. All the way. People have started asking, "Why Skype in the first place? It breaks all the time. Super glitchy. Why not Google Hangouts?" I get it. But here are a few benefits to consider:

First, there are over 300 million Skype users worldwide. 300 million! Can you even fathom that number? I mean, I'm about 70 million years old... if that gives you some perspective. Skype is universal; almost everyone knows how to use it (or can figure it out) and you can connect with almost anyone on the planet. Skype is available for Mac and PC computers, smartphones, tablets and even the XBox!

Second, ever since Microsoft bought the product, they have been working behind the scenes, dramatically improving the quality of Skype. It's improved so dramatically that television stations and studios are now using Skype to replace satellite feeds. What does that mean for us? Better quality over the long haul.

Last, it's FREE! Who doesn't love free?

[M]: I love FREE, Disruptar. And I love Skype too. But if you're still not sure, here's the good news: you can use Google Hangouts. You can use any kind of video strategy you want. But Google Hangouts is still a new player and doesn't have all the bugs worked out and a platform like GotoMeeting, unfortunately, requires a paid subscription. They're more complicated to set up and it's hard to separate the two videos when you're editing which means, it's a lot harder to edit if you mess up an interview.

Now if all this tech-talk has your palms sweating, do not fret! It's easy to produce a high quality audio or video interview but ONLY if you follow the 25 strategies we're about to give you. And honestly, ANY system you use is fine and all of these strategies will work in any interviewing situation.

[D]: That's right, Mike. I may be a Disruptasaurus with a pea-sized brain, but even I understood the importance of following the 25 strategies you teach. Not following them could mean career extinction! Think about it, your interviews will live on the internet for-ev-er. If you don't make the effort to put your best foot forward now, you will regret looking horrible later. These are things that newbies miss. They simply don't notice all the stuff that pros do. If you follow these steps, you can look like a pro from the start.

[M]: That's right, Disruptar. Not to mention, if you *don't* follow these instructions, you could *give* a great interview; provide a lot of great content, wisdom, and position yourself perfectly to catapult into thought-leader-superstardom but get *cut* from the interview because you look bad. What a total shame and it happens all the time. Great voices don't get heard because they look horrible on camera. Don't let that be you! Follow these techniques and soar like an asteroid to great heights!

[D]: Did you have to mention an asteroid, Mike?
[M]: Oh. Sorry, Disruptar. My bad. Let's get to it. I'll take the first one.

Strategy #1: Position Your Camera Lens Above Eye Level

BAD: If your camera is looking UP at you, your audience is looking INTO your nose (who knows what might be in there) and you're going to look FAT because your neck is all scrunched up...

GOOD: When your camera is above your eyes and are looking UP, your neck is extended and you look THIN!

[M]: Let me ask you two questions…

Would you like to lose 10 pounds instantly?

Would you consider it rude if someone you were speaking to insisted you looked straight up their nose?

Hopefully the answer to both of those questions was YES*!*

The most common (huge) mistake I see people make is they do video interviews with their cameras *below* eye level. The result is they look fat, hunched over and old. Worse? The person on the other end winds up counting nose hairs—if they're lucky.

Have you ever watched a bridal party getting their photos taken? Where is the photographer typically standing? Up on top of a bench, or a retaining wall, or hanging from a tree—anything to get above eye level of the subjects. It's the instant diet all brides (and grooms) love because they'll look 10 pounds lighter.

This simple shift of the lens will shave pounds, years and mean you don't have to worry about shaving your nose hairs.

[D]: (Mike, that went too far!)

[M]:*You know it's true, Disruptar.*

Here's the rule: Position your camera lens approximately 1-3 inches (2-6 cm) ABOVE your eyes. If you're using a laptop, just put IT on top of a stack of books or anything that puts it above eye level. If you're using a professional camera or webcam, adjust accordingly.

[D]: Let me jump in here for a second, Mike.

[M]: Of course, Disruptar.

[D]: If you *do* use a stack of books or something, make sure the computer is stable so it doesn't wiggle around or move when you're speaking. Not even a little bit. A shaky or moving lens is amateurish and very annoying to the viewer on the other end.

[M]: Good point, Disruptar. I know wiggly cameras make you feel seasick.

[D]: Yeah, Mike. And they remind me that I can't swim; I got these little arms.

[M]: Ok. Well, there you have it. Mount your camera above eye level and make sure it's stable (especially if you have dinosaur viewers with queasy stomachs).

Strategy #2: Look at the Lens, Not the Screen!

BAD: Don't talk and look at the video of the other person on the monitor

GOOD: Look directly at the camera lens so you maintain eye contact and intimacy

[M]: A very close second to the up-the-nose mistake is this one; amateurs who *think* they're talking to the camera but in reality, all the viewer sees is a buffoon staring off into a distant corner of the screen.

This is a *huge* problem. Not only does it scream rookie, but when someone isn't making eye contact (and in video, you make eye contact with your viewers by looking directly at the camera lens) they appear disconnected, sketchy or just plain creepy. These are *not* the thoughts you want running through your viewers' minds as they watch your video while you do your best to develop trust and rapport.

[D]: Now hold on a second here Mike… it's an honest mistake, isn't it? Looking at the wrong spot on the screen. I mean, you're interviewing someone, they're in a little box on your computer with the other person, isn't it only natural to make eye contact with *them?*

[M]: Yeah, Disruptar, it's true. At first, looking at a tiny lens on a webcam feels a lot less natural than looking at a human on a screen but this is one of those subtle skills that separates a pro from an amateur.

So here's how it's done: Identify your webcam. Got it? Good. Now look at it. The *whole* time. Never stop looking at the webcam. Don't take your eyes off it. For the duration of your interview, act as if your webcam is the most beautiful man or woman in the world. Cool? Make it easier by sliding the preview window of the person you're talking with to directly beneath the camera. As long as it's at eye level and several feet away, it's going to look great. And while you're at it, remind your interviewee, "Look at the camera the whole time. Don't look at the little picture video of me."

Whether you're reminding yourself or your subject, just remember: Eyes on the camera. Always!

Strategy #3: "Frame" Your Shot

BAD: Bad Framing and bad neighbors won't make you look good...

GOOD: It's SHOWTIME and you're the STAR! Make sure the camera knows it.

[M]: Next, framing. The best shots are well-framed. You wouldn't believe how many interviews I watch where one or both people are hanging off the edge of the screen. One person is only showing eyebrows and forehead, the other is only visible chest-to-chin... No one cares what you're saying if they can't see you saying it! After you've set your camera above eye-level and you're sure you're looking at the lens, the next step is to properly position yourself on the screen.

Here are a few rules of thumb:

Make sure you have some head room at the top of the shot. We should be able to *see* the top of your head and a little empty space above it - but don't center your eyes right in the middle of the screen.

Don't cut off any piece of your face or head. I don't care if you have the biggest face in the east, I want to see every last beautiful inch of it!

[D]: Mike, you always tell me to film from the "nipples up." Now, I'm a dinosaur, and I don't really have nipples, but I thought your human viewers would benefit from that tip.

[M]: That's right, Disruptar, as long as you don't have *too* much body showing. Keep your head toward the top of the screen (not in the middle) and you should be good to go!

[D]: And!

[M]: Yes, Disruptar?

[D]: You told me one time to get a big LCD monitor and put it in the background with my logo on it. Gave me cool branding with minimal effort.

[M]: That's right, Disruptar. I often put an LCD monitor on a stand and then show my slides as I speak so they're in the background as well. These are all great ways to reinforce a brand, and it looks really professional too. Framing is important.

[D]: But Mike, what do you do if you don't have a background?

[M]: Good question, Disruptar. If you don't have a much of a background then make sure your head is close to the top of the frame and use a neutral or simple color. There's nothing wrong with a solid white background (like the old Apple commercials).

Always ask yourself, "Where am I?" Don't just be a head in the middle. Try to get your head off to one side or the other, think in thirds, and at the very least put your head up towards the top. We've got high definition, lots of screen, lots of resolution these days. This is how you take advantage of it.

Strategy #4: Backlighting is for Horror Movies!

BAD: This screams HITCHCOCK HORROR! Never shoot with a bright light or window behind you

GOOD: Make sure there's a simple unlit background, not a light behind you

[D]: Yikes!

[M]: What is it, Disruptar?

[D]: That picture looks terrifying!

[M]: Ah. Yes. You're right. It *is* terrifying, isn't it. What's even more terrifying is that this happens all the time in video interviews. People sit in front of a window and the result is something fit for Halloween.

When choosing a background for your interview, remember this: backlights are for horror movies ONLY. Unless you are Alfred Hitchcock and about to be attacked by a demonic flock of birds, make sure you are not setting up your camera facing a window or a bright light. The bright light needs to be on your face, not behind you.

Did you get that? Bright light ON YOUR FACE… NOT behind you.

[D]: I think they got it, Mike. You can turn your Caps lock off.

[M]: Okay. Good. That's tip number four.

Strategy #5: Light from the Front

BAD: Although a "hair light" can look ok, just a single light from the top or sides will result in undesirable shadows which can make you look old or tired.

GOOD: Use any kind of light and point it towards your face, above the camera (but not too close to make your face look shiny)

[D]: So naturally, Mike, if Tip Four is to not have a light behind you, it would make sense that Tip Five is having a light in *front of you*. Go straight to Amazon— you'll be able to get really nice, affordable LED lights that will make you look like a million bucks. Search "web cam lights" and you'll find a variety of great options.

Depending on the strength and type light, you should place it approximately 2-3 feet away from your face.

[M]: That's right Disruptar. The only trick is, you don't want to be *overlit*. You just need good quality lighting that fills up your face without creating glare. And take a close look at yourself to make sure there aren't any big shadows anywhere—sometimes something as simple as a curl in your hair can block the light from your eye or cast a shadow across your cheek.

[D]: Yeah, or your nose could look huge!

[M]: Thanks, Disruptar, for that.

[D]: I only speak the truth, Mike. Just put the light in front of you—even a desk light is better than nothing—and see the difference it makes.

. . . .

Free "Interviewer Buyer's Guide" with Lighting Recommendations

For a copy of Mike's Video Equipment Buyer's Guide with lighting recommendations and links, text your email address to +1 (858) 877-9700 or visit www.Livecasts.net

You'll also receive a step-by-step training video of this book and handy illustrated infographic with every one of these steps that you can print out and post next to your computer or share with someone you want to interview.

. . . .

Strategy #6: Neat, Uncluttered Background

BAD: Dead bodies, bones, nudie dino posters and hostages probably aren't "brand representative" in your interview background

GOOD: A neat, clean nice background

[M]: Okay Disruptar, this is another obvious one but so many people mess this up.

[D]: That's right, Mike. Make sure you have an interesting but uncluttered background. I've seen interviews with people who are supposed to be successful and wealthy, and it looks like they live in a dumpster because there's disarray, stacks of junk and garbage behind them.

If you're in front of a door, close it. Or better yet, make sure your camera is facing a background that will be interesting, attractive and relevant to your audience. Make sure whatever you are in front of is *brand representative*.

[M]: Or cats! Disruptar, do you remember the interview we saw with all the cats walking around?

[D]: I remember that Mike. It was awkward (and made me hungry). Definitely get your animals under control. Unless you're doing an animal show, get them out of your interview environment, and make sure you clean up the place.

[M]: Should we show them the background of one of your early videos, Disruptar?

[D]: Okay fine. Don't judge me—I'm the winner of the Most Improved Background award. But yes, this is a BAD background:

[M]: Don't feel too bad, Disruptar. Again, this is something I've seen so many times. Pay attention to what is in the background. Make sure your background is congruent with your brand. Have something visually interesting and relevant behind you, but not distracting. Now, if you're in the garbage business, it's fine to be Oscar the Grouch and live in a dump. Okay? Other than that, I would recommend that you don't have a bunch of stuff in the background.

[D]: Show them my "after" picture—see? Most Improved.

[M]: Yes, Disruptar. Huge improvement. Nice job.

Strategy #7: Smile! :)

BEFORE.

AFTER.

[M]: Okay. Are you ready for the *cheapest* way to improve your videos??

SMILE!

Smiling is FREE!

I mean, come on. Who would you rather watch, Oscar the Grouch or Kermit the Frog?

Show off those *pearly whites*. Disruptar has a mouthful of them and he shows off every single one! Smiling not only creates happy chemicals inside *your* brain, but people connect and relate to you. In many, many studies that have been conducted on television personalities, the ones who smile the most are liked the most, they're trusted the most and, I would venture to guess, they make the most money.

It might seem strange at first. After all, you're technically talking to a lens on a camera. What about that inspires smiling? It might seem forced or fake, but trust me when I say, the faster you can get over *that*, the faster you'll connect with your viewers. No one wants to buy from Eeyore (the sad donkey in *Winnie the Pooh*), and really, no one wants to *listen* to Eeyore either. Put a smile on your face to create a smile in your voice. It doesn't cost a nickel to smile and the more you do it, the more natural it becomes.

In fact, if you want to do a test, pull out your mobile phone and start an audio recorder. Now record yourself reading - one while you are smiling and another one where you aren't. Now play back the audio and listen carefully. You can actually "hear" a smile and it sounds *profoundly* different.

[D]: Mike, sometimes I print out a big smiley face and then stick it under or alongside my camera to remind myself, "Keep a smile on the whole time".

[M]: Good thinking, Disruptar. Last thing on this: Have you ever scrolled through an interview to try to find an image of yourself that you want to post online? It is *darn* hard to find a still shot that doesn't look horrible, right? All the pros know—anyone who spends a lot of time on stage or in front of a camera—that they need to be striking a pose *all the time*. Why? Because there are always a ton of pictures being taken of them and it's that ugly one that shows up in 'The National Enquirer'. Get it? Maybe you're not prepared for mainstream media right now, but prepare yourself for that opportunity. When people are taking pictures of you, look great as often as you can. (Aka: Smile!)

. . . .

Free Training Video with On-Camera Tips

For a copy of a training video that guides you through each of these strategies and includes on-camera tips and techniques to engage, entertain, educate and thrill your audience, text your email address to +1 (858) 877-9700 or visit www.Livecasts.net

You'll also receive a handy illustrated infographic with every one of these steps that you can print out and post next to your computer or share with someone you want to interview.

. . . .

Strategy #8: Control the Noise

BAD: Your pet pterodactyl is NOT a welcome guest in your interviews.

GOOD: Although we don't recommend taping and tying up your pets, it's critical to control the noise in your environment!

[D]: I've got this one, Mike. Noise.

Babies. I get it. They cry. They giggle. They need stuff. That's fine… just not within earshot of the mic. Same with pets. We already talked about cats wandering in the background, but if you've got a yappy puppy, though I'm sure he's super cute, barking dogs are not cute in an interview. Even worse? You hopping up to say, "Oh, just a second. I've got to run away and put my dog away." If you do that, you'll lose your audience. They'll be asking themselves, "Who is this clown?" It completely degrades the experience and the confidence and trust someone has to have in you. If you can't control your environment, how can you expect your audience to believe you can control and provide good value either?. You will be judged by this.

What are the most common "noise culprits", Mike?

[M]: Well Disruptar, there's a lot to think about when it comes to noise and unless you're an audio engineer, you probably don't even know how much noise is happening all around you.

Body noise. These are the noises you unconsciously make—like sniffeling, snorting, hard breathing, throat-clearing and jewelry.

Room and ambient noise. When you walk into a room, pay attention to subtle whirring or buzzing. Do you have fans that are turning on and off all the time? Air conditioning? A hum from a washing machine on the other side of the wall? Is your computer noisy? How about your chair? Pay attention to your environment. In your day-to-day life you get used to all of these noises, but the sooner you train your mind to listen with "virgin ears", the better your interviews will be.

[D]: Good point, Mike. Luckily, there is a quick tip for preventing some ugly sounding noise when you're doing interviews; set up your microphone with some pillows surrounding it so it doesn't reverberate and bounce. It actually deadens the sound.

But really, the only way to know for sure if you've got a sound issue is to plug your headphones into your device and actually record the background noise (or lack there of). If there is a lot of noise, find a way to control it. For me, I always have a pair of earphones (yes, dinosaurs have ears) in so I can hear everything, including myself. It might drive you a little crazy at first, but it helps develop the sensitivity and awareness to sound that you'll need.

[M]: Oh, before we move on Disruptar, I want to mention one more thing that drives me crazy: Interviewers and interviewees who bang on a desk when they talk. They bump their microphone, tap their fingers on the table, type on their keyboard or folks who wear loose jewelry including bracelets, watches, necklaces or earrings that clink and clang. If it's noisy or can rattle, ring, bang or clank, take it off. Keep your hands in front of you, off the desk or at your sides. If you talk with your hands, don't smack and bang on stuff.

Make the people you interview aware of this as well—because even if you're not banging around but they are, your sound quality will not sound professional.

Fixing audio problems in "post production" is painstaking, time-consuming and expensive. It's best to eliminate the sources of noise in the first place WHILE you record.

Finally, the BEST solution for making sure YOU aren't the source of noise is to make sure you have a MUTE switch on your microphone and use it. If you have a decent microphone, it will have a mute or cough switch. If you're recording with Skype or another software program, there will be a mute software switch you can click when you aren't speaking.

The rule is, if you aren't speaking, mute yourself. And make sure you tell your guest or host to do the same.

Strategy #9: Wrap Your Package

BAD: Um...not!

GOOD: Sweet!

[M]: Now, Disruptar, I hope you don't mind that I tell people we really had to work on this one for you...?

[D]: No Mike. You can tell them.

[M]: One of the biggest things Disruptar was missing in his interviews was this: he wasn't wrapping the package, baby! He wasn't "brand representative" and looked like he just woke up.

(Groggy-dinosaur is not a great look, in case you're wondering.)

You get one first impression, so don't blow it by looking like a slob.

My dad used to tell me, "You act the way you dress." As a kid, I didn't like hearing that and really didn't believe it until I observed it in other people.

Dress for success. Dress for results. Dress for the income you want, not the income you have. People will judge you based on how you present yourself. Unless you're in the garbage business, don't dress in garbage. Put on a nice shirt. Take care of your hair. Brush your teeth for gosh sakes. Look good.

Disruptar always just looked like a doofy, ol' dino. We had to jazz him up a bit to match the jazziness of his message. Once we did that he was golden! If you're a woman, make sure your dress, makeup and accessories are what I call "brand representative". If you're a man, don't be a schlub. Okay?
And if you're whining, "I don't know how to dress," or "I don't know what to wear" or "I don't have anything to wear," then go get someone to dress you. Seriously, if you haven't done this before, I highly recommend you actually go to a client-focused department store like Nordstroms, and ask for someone to help you pick out clothing that match your skin tone, brand, and line of work. It's worth the investment.

I'll never forget the first time I hired someone to dress me. It totally

37

changed how people recognized and even treated me. The first time I wore an ensemble chosen by a professional was the first time, in my entire *life*, I've ever gotten a compliment on my clothing. I mean, I'm from a small town in Minnesota; not really the fashion metropolis of the world…

[D]: You think *you* were style-challenged, Mike?! How do you think I felt? My style is prehistoric. But that investment does make a difference. It'll make a difference in your sales. A more deliberate focus on creating your image, equals more income and revenue for you. Again, we all judge people, so be prepared to be judged.

[M]: Last tip: make sure you wear solid colors; never wear plaids or checkerboard patterns because they'll create "moire" patterns on video. And if you ever wear a lavalier microphone, you should wear a button-up shirt so it can be easily attached and not get bumped or rubbed by clothing or jewelry.

Strategy #10: Create a Memorable Theme

BAD: Plain Jane.

GOOD: Memorable theme.

[M]: All right Disruptar, are you ready to roll?

[D]: What do you mean, Mike?

[M]: We are going to cruise through these next several tips and number ten is to have a theme. In addition to looking good and your first impression, you've got to get and keep your audience's attention by being unique and interesting. Most people decide whether or not they're going to keep watching you in 4-8 seconds. Your goal is to get them to stick around for at least 30 seconds so you can get to the "what's in it for them" part of the interview.

Maybe it's a costume, or a spiel, or a wacky hook. Why? Because most interviews are yawn-city and for that reason, even if there *is* valuable content, no one learns anything because they can't stay awake long enough to watch it.

If you have just a little theme that represents what you're going to be talking about—something you can act out—you will stand out among the hundreds of others who were not brave enough to do it.

It could be the background. It could be a costume that you open up with, or some sort of a tchotchke, but having a theme for an interview means you will be memorable.

[D]: Mike, this is really how I made a name for myself. I'm infamous for disrupting the norm and delivering something the audience will watch and remember.

[M]: Yes Disruptar, you sure are right about that (on more levels than I care to explain right now). No matter what, remember this: You are in the attention-getting business. If that isn't absolutely clear to you, it's going to come back later and bite you with its big dinosaur teeth. Your success depends on whether or not you can get and keep people's attention. A memorable theme is an easy way to do it.

Strategy #11: Use Props

BAD: Derrrr....boring...

GOOD: Tada! Make every moment in your interview interesting and magical!

[D]: Let's talk about props, Mike. You love props!

[M]: You're right Disruptar, I do! I frequently have props that are both interesting and relevant to what I'm talking about and I know the audience will love. Once it was a giant stack of money, I've used a crystal ball, and even a real live Pug Dog!

[D]: A Pug, Mike?

[M]: Yep. A Pug.

[D]: I thought pets were a no-go.

[M]: They are, Disruptar… unless they're a prop! Get, use and talk about your props and use them as metaphors for your presentation, speech or sales strategy. It's a fun way to liven things up, to keep people's attention and to keep them guessing—what the heck is this guy gonna do next?? Especially in video interviewing, being able to talk about a prop—holding them, holding them up to the camera—it creates a depth of visual interest. Now they're not just interested in you, but in your topic, the interview itself *and* the way you're presenting the material.

They're also a great way to "open loops"— that's an NLP or "Neuro Linguistic Programming" term. Humans always want to feel as though we've reached a state of completion. Therefore, if someone sees a prop and you say, "In a moment we're going to talk about this diddly-doo and why it's important", they'll likely stick around to find out what that diddly-doo is and what it does.

Props are also excellent metaphors—when you can illustrate a complex idea or subject with a visually-interesting prop, you'll have a higher likelihood of being able to communicate your ideas in a way that appeals to every type of learning style.

[D]: You're getting pretty fancy right now Mike.
[M]: Sorry, Disruptar. But like you said, I love props!

Strategy #12: Prepare a Bio

BAD: YOU are IMPORTANT! Make sure the interviewer and audience knows it!

GOOD: Give you host some options, let them tell you story the way YOU want it told!

[D]: Okay Mike, I heard you talk about having pre-prepared bio and at first I thought it sounded a little braggy or presumptuous.

[M]: Presumptuous, ay? That's a pretty big word for you, Disruptar.

[D]: I'm not just a pretty face, Mike. But as I was saying, I quickly learned the value of this easily-overlooked strategy when one day I was asked to be interviewed as an attention-getting guru (which I am). Unfortunately, when the guy introduced me, he didn't say anything about my mad-attention-getting-skillz; instead told some stupid joke about a dinosaur walking into a bar.

[M]: Yeah, Disruptar; I hate to say it but this happens all the time. If you're being interviewed, you really can't count on the interviewer to do you justice unless you do the work for them ahead of time. If you want someone to put *your* best foot forward and not screw it up, you gotta write an intro *for* them.

Here's what I've done. I have a bio. It's in Google Docs. Before I am going to do an interview with someone, I share that document with them. In it, there's a long bio. There's a medium bio. There's a short bio. I have bio bullets. I have my whole backstory. I have links to previous interviews. Quotes. Hooks. References to celebrities I've worked with. Pictures. Speaking topics. Links to my social media accounts. Links to my books and products. Basically anything they could possibly need, I give them up front. That way, the person can get as prepared as possible without actually doing any preparation whatsoever. I'll say, "Scroll down to the short bio and read that." Boom. Now you're having someone introduce you on *your* terms.

What typically happens if you're dealing with an amateur interviewer (and even some pros), is right before you start the interview they'll say something like, "Hey. I didn't have time to get prepared. Can you give me three or four bullet points on what you want me to say to get this thing rolling?" I guarantee you, they're going to make you sound like a schmuck. Okay?

[D]: It's sad but true, Mike. This definitely happened to me. Don't suffer the same fate I did! If you're being interviewed, you want the interviewer to read YOUR version of your bio, not theirs. And if you're interviewing someone, ask for the same and do it in advance. It'll make your job easier and make them look better. Win-win-win!

[M]: What's the third win, Disruptar?

[D]: There isn't one Mike. I just wanted to get your attention. Heh heh.

[M]: Very funny, Disruptar.

· ·

Free Copy of Mike's Bio and Speaker Introduction

For a copy of Mike's most recent bio to use as an example you can model and send to interviewers, text your email address to +1 (858) 877-9700 or visit www.Livecasts.net

You'll also receive a step-by-step training video of this book and handy illustrated infographic with every one of these steps that you can print out and post next to your computer or share with someone you want to interview.

· ·

Strategy #13: Open with a Story

BAD: Who are you? Why should the audience care about you and what you have to share??

GOOD: Use an opening story to turn YOU into a MOVIE or a BOOK about YOU that they want to watch or read!

[M]: All right Disruptar, tell me. What is the easiest way to win over an audience in less than a minute?

[D]: That's easy Mike. Open up your interview with a compelling story! Make your opening sentence, "Let me tell you a story…" The human brain (and a dinosaur brains too, I guess) is programmed to respond and listen to stories—it's how we learn. They won't be able to resist you.

Have a story that's relevant, that is germane to the theme, and ties in your bio and the topic being discussed. For example, if Mike were being interviewed about being interviewed and discussing how to look great with online video interviews with Skype or Google Hangouts… A great story to start with is the one about Peter Diamandis.

He would tell you that he had this great opportunity to interview someone he really, really liked, admired and wanted to be associated and affiliated with. Then he would tell you that because of timing, he compromised his location and made a bad decision that ended up making him, (the guy who's supposed to be a video expert) look bad.

He would say if he had to do it all over again, here's what he'd have done differently, and that he's going to make sure you don't suffer the same fate.

[M]: Hey Disruptar, isn't that kind of what we did at the beginning of this book?

[D]: Glad you're finally catching on, Mike. Anytime you can share a story that shows your weakness, your personal journey, or what we call your 'Origin story', where you came from and where you are today, and how you're going to take the audience there with you, you create an instant relationship with a viewer.

Also, please note that I said, "Let me tell *you* a story…" This is extremely important.
The most powerful word in the English language is YOU.

When you are recording your interviews and talking to your audience, talk as though you are talking to *one person*. Not a bunch of people, not a group of people. *Never* say, "Hey you guys", "folks" or say "all of you" in an interview. Remember, unless your viewer plans "interview-watching-parties" (which no one has done in the history of the Internet), they're likely watching the video by themselves. Speak as though you are speaking to *ONE PERSON*.

[**M**]: Not to mention, Disruptar, the women in your audience probably don't like being called "you guys."

[**D**]: Right Mike. So remember, tell a story and tell it like you're telling it to one person. Doing this creates a really special level of connection and intimacy that is broken the moment you start talking as if they're a group or audience.

Strategy #14: Never Point

BAD: Would you poke a baby in the eye?

GOOD: Probably not. Never point at the camera. Use your hands and arms to show you care about them!

[M]: Let me ask you, Disruptar; how do you feel when someone pokes you?

Or points at your face?

Or waves their fingers within inches of your eyes?

[D]: Uhhhh, like I want to bite those fingers off??

[M]: Exactly. That's what you're doing if you point directly at the camera. Because the distance between the viewer and their screen is usually a short one, when you point a finger at them, your finger is only three inches from their face!

Your finger can be a weapon. Don't use it on your innocent viewers. They don't deserve that kind of mistreatment. What have they ever done to you??

Every time you feel a pointing urge coming on, I want you to imagine that you're about to stab a baby in the eye.

[D]: Whoa, Mike. That's a little harsh, don't you think?

[M]: You bet it's harsh! Why am I being so harsh about this? Because pointing within inches of someone's face could be a dangerous act (especially if you point at a Disruptasaurus). You don't point at people that you care about or love.

Another gesture to avoid: finger templing. Never temple your fingers. This is a subconscious or overt sign of superiority from the speaker's perspective that's saying "I'm better or smarter than you." Politicians do this when they're speaking to someone they don't respect. There's a natural reaction most people have to "reel away" from this posture. As a result, it breaks intimacy, trust and connection with your audience.

Avoid "templing" - it's a sign the speaker thinks they're superior and creates distance between the audience.

These are subtle mistakes, but when you commit *hand-crimes*, your viewers sense the barriers they create. They sense the "I am better than you" undertone. We notice and feel it. It feels wrong. It's like putting up a concrete barrier between the connection we have with each other.

Use open gestures. Arms that are inviting. Think big, warm, virtual hugs. Don't put up hand barriers. Don't poke at people. It's not nice.

Strategy #15: Fifteen Minute Rule

BAD: Don't you hate it when you forget what to say or aren't prepared for a meeting or speech and your audience is staring at you with a blank look in their faces?

GOOD: It only takes 15 minutes to look and sound sharp when you follow the 15 minute rule!

[D]: I got this one, Mike. This one is easy. Follow the 15 Minute Rule. What does that mean?

Fifteen minutes before your interview, get prepared and run through everything you want to accomplish and do in your interview in your head. Drink a big glass of water. Get your props set up and next to you. Sit your butt down in your chair. Grab whatever kind of show notes you have, review them and Imagine yourself being interviewed. Think about your theme. Think about the story you're going to open with. Start smiling. Imagine how you're going to make the viewer smile, laugh, cry or feel.

If you can get prepared a half an hour before, even better.

[M]: I'll add, Disruptar, that I prepare the night before... just to be sure. I go to sleep with the interview seeded in my head because I often wake up with a fresh perspective or set of ideas I can use. Mostly,I hate surprises and making mistakes, especially when they're preventable.

[D]: Way to show off, Mike.

Strategy #16:
Restart Your Computer!

BAD: Nothing is worse than having your computer crash in the middle of an interview - especially if it's LIVE! :(

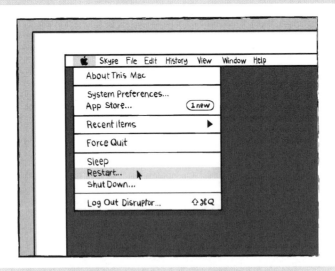

GOOD: The solution? Restart BEFORE the interview begins!

[M]: Oh! Disruptar, this goes with what you were just saying about the 15 minute preparation…

Make sure you restart your computer!
Shortly before the interview, shutdown and restart.

Computers have a nasty reputation of crashing at inopportune times, especially if they've been running for days or weeks without a break.

Chances are, you're likely running a bunch of apps you don't even know you're running. Web browsers are notorious for being giant memory hogs and cause "leaks" that wind up slowing down your computer which can affect the audio and video quality of your interview.

Restart. Clean the slate. The last thing you need is for your computer to freeze up when you're in the middle of an emotionally-charged story and after you've built a great connection with the interviewer or interviewee.

It's hard to get back into that state or edit two chunks of an interview together, especially because this is an extremely preventable problem to solve.

Strategy #17: Test Your Connection Speed

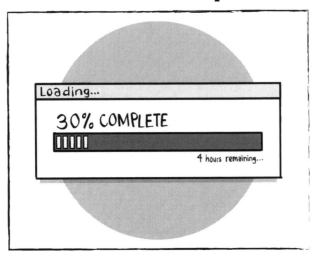

BAD: Slow connections cause horrible audio and video problems that make YOU look and sound bad...

GOOD: Get the fastest connection you can afford and connect your computer directly to your router with a cable for the best quality possible. Wifi is not an interviewer's best friend...

[D]: I gotta admit Mike. Before we met, my internet speed was prehistoric.

Entire civilizations could rise and fall by the time my computer loaded a page.

And video?! Forget it.

[M]: You'd be shocked how many people still live this way, Disruptar. If you are reading this and have not upgraded your internet speed to the fastest you can afford, then do it *immediately*. Fast connections will always make you more money than you spend.

[D]: That's right, Mike. Think of it this way: the more stuff you can get done, the faster you can get it done, the more money you make. But if you're working with a slow internet connection, there's a high probability your audio is going to sound horrible, your video is going to look unprofessional, and that makes you look like *you're ready for extinction*. We've been talking a lot about the fact that, like it or not, people are going to judge you and that includes the speed and the quality of your audio and video. ROAR!

[M]: I'm not even mad that you're getting worked up about this, Disruptar. People should be mad about slow internet that steals their most precious asset—*their time*. There are speed tests available online—all you gotta do is go to Google and search for 'Internet speed test'. Check your connection speed.

One other tip: Whenever possible, connect your computer directly to your router with a cable. It's sad but Wifi is not live video's friend. It can be degraded by interference, mirrors or microwaves.

Strategy #18:
Turn Off File Sharing

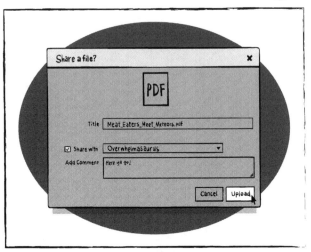

BAD: File sharing can cause hiccups, glitches, jerky video and audio problems.

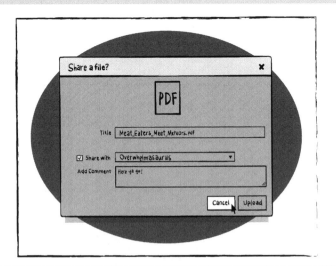

GOOD: By turning off file sharing and downloads and letting everyone on your network know you have an interview scheduled, you'll get a quality recording.

[M]: This one is easy.

Don't share files when you do interviews.

[D]: Duh.

[M]: File sharing on a home or office network shows down your internet connection and can make your audio or video sound or look horrible. Turn it off.

Still not clear what that means? Make sure your computer and every computer on your network are not downloading files while you're doing an interview. If you're on a shared connection, let everyone know when you're about to do an interview so they can stop the downloads until after you're done.

Strategy #19: No Uploads

BAD: Uploading files are even worse than downloads for your interviews and recordings. Turn them all off.

GOOD: Make sure you pause backups, uploads and notify everyone on your network of scheduled interviews.

[M]: Just as a tyrannosaurus is to a small herbivore, uploads are one of the biggest enemies of any audio or video interview. In fact, they're worse than downloads.

[D]: *I'm a little offended by that, Mike.*

[M]: *Sorry Disruptar, but it's true.* Once you've restarted your computer and made sure nobody is sharing files on your network, make sure you keep all unnecessary applications turned off. Even a web browser is a potential liability for causing audio or video glitches to occur.

BitTorrent sharing, FTP uploads, automatic backup operations, extra apps, clicks or actions can affect your sound or your video quality.

Most internet connections have much slower upload than download speeds. And for you, the upload speed is actually MORE important than download speeds. So anything that is hogging your connection can harm the quality of your recording stream.

Strategy #20: In-Ear Monitor

BAD: Don't be a dork. Headsets make you look like you live in your grandmother's basement and play video games all day.

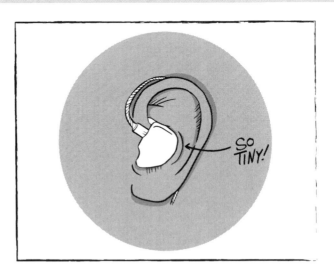

SO TINY!

GOOD: Pros wear in-ear monitors. They're tiny and invisible when worn correctly.

[M]: If you're planning to do interviews, one of the first pieces of equipment you're going to need to invest in is an in-ear-monitor. Now, I know what you might be thinking, "Mike, an in-ear-monitor is more expensive! Can't I just get a pair of headphones and get the same result?"

To that I answer: In terms of sound, probably. In terms of look, branding, and customer perception? Well… you tell me?

Take a look at your before picture, Disruptar. You look like a 24-hour gamer nerd that lives in his grandmother's basement. That might be fine if that's your brand or if nobody sees you… but you're on camera! Unless your brand is "Dufus Who Lives in His Grandmother's Basement," a headset is not "brand representative."

Now take a look at the in-ear monitor… you can barely even see that thing! That's what you're going for. If you want to look like a respectable, branded professional AND record an interview that's television-worthy you've got to get an in-ear monitor. There's just no way around it.

There are a lot of different models—the cheapest ones like the one you see below are as low as $10 and the super fancy ones can go over $1,000. The simple ones are the same headsets you see security guards wearing.

You'll need an extension cable for it, but just plug them into your

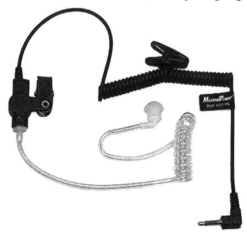

computer jack, clip it into your ears, snaps on to the back of your shirt and wah-la! Super pro vs. super dork!

[D]: Yeah, that all sounds great Mike, but what if you have teeny-tiny-dino-ears like me?

[M]: Lucky for you, Disruptar, there are speciality shops that do custom orders! That's what the broadcasters and musicians use; custom in-ear monitors. I've got a pair right here from a company called 'Ultimate Ears' or 'Gorilla Ears'. Search on Google for "In Ear Monitor" or one of the brands I just mentioned.

For custom in-ear monitors, you go to an audiologist. They make custom molds so you get a monitor that you can wear for an entire day at a time. (The cheap ones get annoying or agitate in your ear after an hour or two.)

What's important is, *remember*, you are there to put on a good show and to *look good*, so you're packaging and your presentation is valuable. Unless you live in your grandmother's basement and you live on pb&j sandwiches, I'd recommend investing in an in-ear monitor that serves you and your brand.

Free In-Ear Monitor "Gear Guide"

For up-to-date links of the in-ear monitors and other interview gear Mike recommends and uses, text your email address to +1 (858) 877-9700 or visit www.Livecasts.net

You'll also receive a step-by-step training video of this book and handy illustrated infographic with every one of these steps that you can print out and post next to your computer or share with someone you want to interview.

Strategy #21:
High-Quality Microphone

BAD: Your built-in microphone picks up ambient noise and won't sound professional.

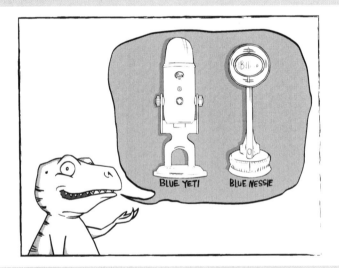

GOOD: There are fantastic USB microphones for less than $100 that are as good as the mics used on radio and TV.

[D]: And while they're at it Mike, don't you think they should skip the built-in microphone inside their computer?

[M]: I'm telling you, a good microphone will cost you less than $100 while a bad microphone (aka: the one currently built into your computer) will cost you *thousands* in sales and potentially *millions* in lost opportunities. A bad microphone simply creates a significantly lower quality recording.

[D]: Mike, I know when I was just getting started I was having a lot of challenges with my audio. My voice is all over the place and my built-in microphone couldn't handle the range. I was blasting people with distortion. *Roar!*

[M]: I can just imagine, Disruptar. And many humans have the same challenge too. I recommend checking out either a Blue Nessie, which costs about $70 on Amazon, or a Blue Yeti. They cost around $100. The Blue Nessie sounds great and connects seamlessly with an in-ear monitor with a built-in connector.

To make buying a microphone and other equipment painless, I've included a link to my free "Interviewer Gear Guide" when you respond to the "Call to Action" box below.

· ·

Free Microphone "Gear Guide"

For up-to-date links of the microphones and other interview equipment Mike recommends and uses, text your email address to +1 (858) 877-9700 or visit www.Livecasts.net

You'll also receive a step-by-step training video of this book and handy illustrated infographic with every one of these steps that you can print out and post next to your computer or share with someone you want to interview.

· ·

Strategy #22: Get a High-Quality Webcam or Camera

BAD: Although it's "better than nothing", your built-in webcam won't look as good as an external webcam or video camera.

GOOD: Starting as low as $100 will get you a really nice webcam that looks 3 times better than your built-in camera.

[M]: We're getting close to the end, Disruptar.

[D]: We sure are—these are the last but certainly not the least. I mean, what great web interview doesn't start with a great webcam or camera?

[M]: That's right, my friend! The built-in camera that comes with most computers and laptops these days is *pretty good*. However, if you *can*, you might as well get the top of the line. The hottest camera right now, as we write this book, is the Logitech webcam — the C930e. This thing looks awesome, and if it's lit properly, most people can't tell that it isn't a $2,000 professional camera.

[D]: And it's portable, too Mike!

[M]: That's right Disruptar. You can take it with you and do interviews while you're visiting your family in Wichita.

You do get what you pay for and free is great. But for about $100 or so, the Logitech webcam is a fantastic deal for the money. To get the next level in quality, you need to connect a camcorder ($300 and up) and get a computer interface that costs between $150-$300. (That option does give you a noticeable improvement in quality but it's a significant jump in cost.)

. . . .

Free Webcam and Camera "Gear Guide"

For up-to-date links of the cameras and other equipment Mike recommends and uses for interviews, text your email address to +1 (858) 877-9700 or visit www.Livecasts.net

You'll also receive a step-by-step training video of this book and handy illustrated infographic with every one of these steps that you can print out and post next to your computer or share with someone you want to interview.

. . . .

Strategy #23:
Record the Interview

BAD: What would happen if the interviewer's computer crashed during your best performance?

GOOD: Call Recorder software to the rescue! Both the interviewer and interviewee should record - just in case something goes wrong.

[M]: Here's a riddle for you Disruptar: If an interview happens in the woods and it isn't recorded, *did the interview ever really happen?*

[D]: Uhhhh….

[M]: While he thinks about that… let me tell you some inside info about the industry's favorite call recorders. There are a couple of different products available.

The one I use for the Macintosh is called 'eCamm Call Recorder'. I've been using it for years and years. It is pretty flawless. And with a $20 price tag, you really can't go wrong. It records both sides of the video, also both sides of the audio, so it can be mixed and edited later on by a professional.

If you are a PC user, you'll want to check out the one from Pamela or the one from VodBurner. All you have to do is look up 'Skype Call Recorder' in Google, and a whole bunch of them are going to show up… I always recommend to test before you buy.

Whether you're the interviewer or interviewee, I recommend you always record your interview in case something goes wrong. I've done lots of interviews where the interviewer has said, "Oh man, I'm really sorry. My recording software just crashed and I lost everything." My response was, "That's ok. I've got a recording and I'll send it right over."

It's very cool to be a lifesaver.

Secondly, just about every interviewee wants a copy of the interview and asks for it when it's over. Why not just be prepared and do it yourself? The interviewer has a LOT on their plate and remembering to send you a copy of the interview might not be at the top of their priority list.

Free Call Recorder Guide

For up-to-date links of the call recorder software Mike recommends and uses, text your email address to +1 (858) 877-9700 or visit www.Livecasts.net

You'll also receive a step-by-step training video of this book and handy illustrated infographic with every one of these steps that you can print out and post next to your computer or share with someone you want to interview.

Strategy #24:
Interact with the Audience!

BAD: Your audience is distracted...texting, Twittering, Twaddling, Facebooking or Instagramming - which means you're not going to be memorable and they're not going to remember what you say

GOOD: Give your audience something to do or write down to keep them engaged. Tell them what to do and they'll do it!

[D]: I have to say… of all the secrets you taught me Mike, this is the best one. BE INTERACTIVE! Even if your interview isn't live, you want it to *feel* as though it's live. And the way you do that is to be interactive. Ideally, you'll "embed" direct actions the listener or viewer can do during and after the interview is completed.

You want your interview to be timeless and relevant anytime, anywhere and on any device.

[M]: I'm not going to lie Disruptar, this can be a difficult one to master… but those who do are the ones who become "interview-famous." Here's an example of how I do this:

I often say throughout my videos or interviews, "If you're listening to me or watching me right now, grab a pen (I will pick up and hold a pen close to the camera lens) and, I want you to grab a piece of paper or open up your notebook and write this down…"

Anytime you directly look into the camera and ask an audience to do something, they will very likely do it if you've built rapport with them.

By giving them directives and commands, they're going to pay much closer attention to you. If you say, "Don't miss out on this. You're going to want to write this down. This is the kind of thing that you're going to regret later if you don't write this down right now…." Your viewers will respond to that—as long as you deliver on your promises.

If you monetize your interviews by turning them into podcasts and have sponsors, advertisers or sell your own products, training your audience to pay attention and take action will make your tribe significantly more valuable.

[D]: And Mike, let's not forget how distracted everyone is! This is my specialty. If they're not *interacting* with you, it means they're likely interacting with someone else on text or Twittering or Twaddling or Facebooking instead of paying attention to you. You've got to *disrupt* their distractions by getting them to interact. ROAR!

[M]: Disruptar… are you done on your soap box?

[D]: Yes, Mike. I think I am.

. . . .

Read This: It's a CTA (Call To Action)

At the end of many of the chapters in this book is a "Call To Action" in a box like this one.

It's an example of what you want to embed in every marketing, training content or interview you give your audience. It' an opportunity to go deeper with you and your products to build rapport, trust and create a connection. They need to see YOU and your products as a solution to their problems.

For a step-by-step training video of this book and a handy illustrated infographic with every one of these steps that you can print out and post next to your computer or share with someone you want to interview, text your email address to +1 (858) 877-9700 or visit www.Livecasts.net

. . . .

Strategy #25: No Sound Effects

BAD: Don't annoy your listener or viewer with random sound effects, noises, dings, dongs, boops, beeps, clangs, woots, buzzes and changles.

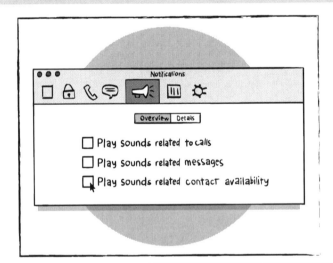

GOOD: Turn off sound effects. All of them. Including your phone. One random noise can ruin the intimacy and connection you've spent time building with your interviewer and audience.

[M]: YOU MADE IT! We're at the end. The final tip for getting attention and making your interviews look and sound professional.

[D]: What is it Mike?! What's the last tip!

[M]: This is an easy one, Disruptar. But what's easy to do is often easily overlooked.

First, let me ask you this: How do you feel when you have a guest over for dinner who looks at their phone all evening? How would you like it if they took calls in the middle of dinner and left every message notification on so you could hear every text message and email as it came in? Would that make you feel important and prioritized? Would it make your dinner intimate and connected?

[D]: NO!

[M]: That's right, Disruptar. Do your viewers a favor and PUT. The PHONE. DOWN! Turn off your computer sounds, phone and other noisemakers while you do your interview. Especially Skype notifications. Dings, dongs, bings, woots, buzzes and boops make you appear very unprofessional and amateurish.

And worse… if you're a guest, your host will probably not want you back. You'll ruin the interview.

If you do interviews with Skype, go to Preferences > Notifications > Overview and turn them all off.

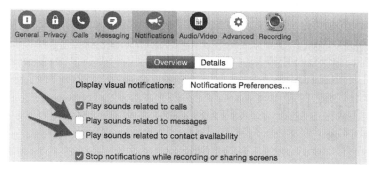

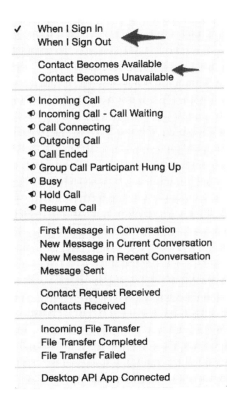

[D]: Sometimes I really like turning my notifications off, Mike.

[M]: Yeah?

[D]: ...because when I turn them back on and there are so many, I feel really special.

[M]: You *are* special Disruptar!

[D]: Thanks, Mike. So are you.

Summary of the Strategies

[M]: There you have it! Those are the *25 Strategies to Make Your YouTube, Livestream, Google Hangouts, Skype Interviews and Videos Look or Sound Like a Professional TV or Radio Show.*

[D]: Mike, I think it's time for a quick review and a "call to action"...

[M]: Go for it, Disruptar—we want you to start making great video interviews as quickly as possible.

[D]: That's right! So number #1 is to respond to one of the CTA - "Call To Action" boxes in this book and get the training video, infographic and Interview Buyer's Guide to get the right equipment that's always up to date.

Next, for just a few dollars, get yourself all the tech-stuff we talked about (lights, in-ear monitor, microphone, and even webcam) as soon as possible. Look like a professional. It makes a big difference.

Next, review this checklist before you do any kind of an interview. And make sure you send it to anyone you're interview as well. It doesn't do anyone any good if half the interview team looks pro and the other half looks like a hot mess.

Then, TAKE ACTION! Book an interview! Just get started. There are so many ways you can use interviews to build your brand. You can create a book from an interview. You can create articles. You can create podcasts. You can create any kind of marketing or promotional content, and you can use them to elevate your brand by associating with other experts and authorities.

If you take the time to do each one of these, even people who have been conducting interviews for years will watch your videos and wonder how on earth you got so good, so quickly!

[M]: Great review, Disruptar! And he's right. If you just do these 25 things… even if you've never recorded an interview before in your life… you will look and sound like a television or radio pro. And when you look like a pro, people will treat you like a pro; which means more credibility, more views, and most importantly more money for the products and services you offer. I speak for both myself and Disruptar when I say congrats in advance for your next professional quality video.

[D] [M]: ROAR!

Books by Mike Koenigs

Author Expert Marketing Machines: *The Ultimate 5-Step, Push-Button, Automated System to Become the Expert, Authority and Star in Your Niche*

Make Market Launch IT: *The Ultimate Product Creation System for Turning Your Ideas Into Income*

Podcast Strategies: *How to Podcast – 21 Questions Answered*

Multicast Marketing: *How to Podcast, Publish and Promote Your Content to the World with Google Hangouts, YouTube Live, Kindle Books and Social Media*

Top Gun Consulting: *How to Create a Fun and Lucrative Business Sharing Your Knowledge, Experience or Story*

You Everywhere Now: *Get Your Message, Products and Services in Front of Your Target Prospects and in Every Pocket, Screen, Car and Television in the World with the Help of the Largest Brands*

Publish and Profit: *A 5-Step System for Attracting Paying Coaching and Consulting Clients, Traffic and Leads, Product Sales and Speaking Engagements*

How to Be a Video Interview Pro: *25 Strategies to Get ATTENTION and Make Your YouTube, Livestream, Google Hangouts, Skype Interviews and Videos Look or Sound Like a Professional TV or Radio Show*

Programs and Products
by Mike Koenigs

Quickly start your own online interactive TV show or infomercial channel to build an audience, list, promote your products, services or brand even if you aren't a techie. The ultimate video marketing system for entrepreneurs, small business owners, authors, experts, speakers, coaches, consultants and creatives.

What is the "Livecast Profit Toolkit"?

Have you ever watched an infomercial on TV or online and wondered how they're made and whether or not one could be made about your products, services or you and sell your products in a highly interactive and educational way to make money for you without having to sell in person, on stage and at little or no expense?

What if it was easy to do and took just a couple of hours to get started with equipment you already own and know how to use?

The Livecast Profit Toolkit is a live and online training course that teaches entrepreneurs, small business owners, authors, experts, speakers, coaches, consultants and creative types how to start their own *Interactive Online Television Shows* to sell products and services.

"Livecasts" are just like TV infomercials except they are interactive and can be produced and broadcast for free using equipment you already own and know how to use. The Livecast Profit Toolkit teaches you how to use low-cost computers and camera equipment and produce a compelling, educational, entertaining business show that gets viewers interested in any product or service.

. . . .

Visit:
www.LivecastToolkit.com for a free video and more information.

. . . .

Join Me for a Free Online Training Workshop!

Let's Connect!

Every month I do a free online training workshop to teach and share the latest "what's working now" strategies to build your audience, grow your list, rapidly create products and services with proven online interactive video systems.

· ·

To get regular workshop invitations, updates and a copy of a video version of this book text your email address to +1 (858) 877-9700 or visit www.Livecasts.net

· ·

Book Mike to Speak!

Book Mike Koenigs as your Keynote Speaker and You're Guaranteed to Make Your Event Highly Entertaining and Unforgettable!

For over two decades, Mike Koenigs has been educating, entertaining and helping entrepreneurs, authors, experts, speakers, consultants and coaches build and grow their businesses with the online video, social media, mobile and product creation strategies.

His backstory includes his recent near-death brush with stage 3a cancer, growing up lower middle-class in a small town in Eagle Lake Minnesota, severe ADHD and "meeting" Tony Robbins through an infomercial that changed his life forever. After successfully building and exiting from two companies and selling them to publicly-traded companies, Mike can share relevant, actionable strategies that anyone can use - even if they're starting from scratch.

His unique style inspires, empowers and entertains audiences while giving them the tools and strategies they need and want to get seen, heard, build and grow successful sustainable brands and businesses.

· ·

For more info, visit www.MikeKoenigs.com/speaking or call +1 (858) 412-0858.

Made in the USA
San Bernardino, CA
28 July 2015